Sound Advice on

MIDI Production

by Bill Gibson

ProAudio
p r e s s

236 Georgia Street, Suite 100
Vallejo, CA 94590
(707) 554–1935

Publisher: Mike Lawson
Art Director: Stephen Ramirez; Editor: Patrick Runkle

Cover image courtesy Midas.

ProAudio Press is an imprint of artistpro.com, LLC
236 Georgia Street, Suite 100
Vallejo, CA 94590
(707) 554-1935

Also from ProMusic Press
Music Copyright for the New Millennium
The Mellotron Book
Electronic Music Pioneers

Also from EMBooks
The Independent Working Musician
Making the Ultimate Demo, 2nd Ed.
Remix: The Electronic Music Explosion
Making Music with Your Computer, 2nd Ed.
Anatomy of a Home Studio
The EM Guide to the Roland VS-880

Also from MixBooks
The AudioPro Home Recording Course, Volumes I, II, and III
The Art of Mixing: A Visual Guide to Recording, Engineering, and Production
The Mixing Engineer's Handbook
The Mastering Engineer's Handbook
Music Publishing: The Real Road to Music Business Success, Rev. and Exp. 5th Ed.
How to Run a Recording Session
The Professional Musician's Internet Guide
The Songwriters Guide to Collaboration, Rev. and Exp. 2nd Ed.
Critical Listening and Auditory Perception
Modular Digital Multitracks: The Power User's Guide, Rev. Ed.
Professional Microphone Techniques
Sound for Picture, 2nd Ed.
Music Producers, 2nd Ed.
Live Sound Reinforcement
Professional Sound Reinforcement Techniques
Creative Music Production: Joe Meek's Bold Techniques

Printed in Auburn Hills, MI
ISBN 1-931140-28-6

Contents

MIDI Theory

Though MIDI is somewhat old news for a third millennium book, it still pertains directly to the operation of many current and forthcoming mixers and processors. Not only do many digital audio software packages use MIDI parameters to control mixdown, but many hardware mixers use MIDI to automate and control all audio parameters—sequenced and digitally recorded.

With an understanding of the information in this book, you should be able to easily and willingly tackle any MIDI equipment you'll encounter. There are no mysteries to MIDI. The system is logical and powerful.

The Language

MIDI has been the fundamental Musical Instrument Digital Interface since the early '80s. It behooves us to understand the communication principles involved in

MIDI data transfer, even as newer and more improved formats evolve.

MIDI is nothing more than a common language used by synthesizers, sound modules, and any other MIDI-implemented instrument to communicate either with each other or with a hardware- or software-based MIDI sequencer. A MIDI interface is simply an interpreter to assist in communications between the MIDI instrument and a computer.

The communication language is based on a hexadecimal (16-digit) binary code. In other words, each parameter and function of a MIDI device is represented by a unique arrangement of 16 1s and 0s. Middle C on the synthesizer keyboard is assigned a unique and specific binary number. Anytime that note is played, its unique binary code is transmitted from the MIDI OUT port. That code is then received by another synth through the MIDI IN port. When the synth recognizes the unique binary code for middle C it, too, plays middle C. This process takes about three milliseconds.

MIDI Communication

Anytime a note is played or a controller is used, its unique binary code is transmitted from the MIDI OUT port. That code is then received by another synth through the MIDI IN port. When the synth recognizes the unique binary code for whatever MIDI parameter has been transmitted, it, too, responds to the command. This process takes about three milliseconds.

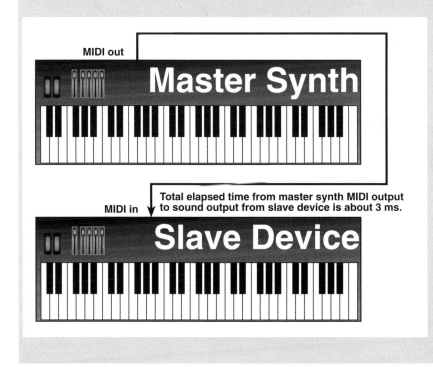

MIDI out

Master Synth

MIDI in → Total elapsed time from master synth MIDI output to sound output from slave device is about 3 ms.

Slave Device

This simple concept is applied to each MIDI parameter, forming a powerful and musically efficient means of communication in the electronic music genre. The list of MIDI controllable parameters is extensive, ranging from note value to portamento value to poly/mono/omni mode selection.

MIDI program developers have adopted many terms common to analog signal processing. Most programs give you the option to create delays, compression, echoes, arpeggios, choruses, and more. The controls have come to resemble a piece of hardware rather then a box full of numbers.

MIDI Ports

There are typically three MIDI port on the back of a MIDI device: MIDI IN, MIDI OUT, and MIDI THRU. A 5-pin DIN connector and jack are used to interconnect MIDI devices.

MIDI Connection

To connect MIDI equipment together, connect the MIDI OUT of the controlling device (Master) to the MIDI IN of the device being controlled (Slave). Once this connection has been successfully completed, the pathway is clear for communication. Remember, MIDI cables carry controlling data only. They don't carry audio signals.

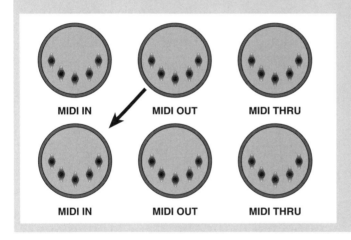

MIDI IN, OUT, and THRU

There are typically three MIDI port on the back of a MIDI device: MIDI IN, MIDI OUT, and MIDI THRU.

To connect MIDI equipment together, connect the MIDI OUT of the controlling device to the MIDI IN of the device being controlled. Once this connection has been successfully completed, the pathway is clear for communication.

MIDI Cables

MIDI cables use a standard 5-pin DIN connector. The cable is similar to a mic cable in that it utilizes a twisted pair of conductors, surrounded by a shield. Even though the connector has five pins, only three are in use for the standard MIDI format. Pins 1 and 3 (the outer two pins) are not connected in the classic MIDI cable—they're left for future development and manufacturer-specific design. Pin 2 is connected to the shield for ground, and pins 4 and 5 are used to conduct the MIDI data.

It's even possible to make adapter cables with the 5-pin DIN connector on one end and a standard XLR connector on the other. Since both standards only use three pins, there's no loss when converting to XLR. Simply connect pin 2 of the DIN connector to pin 1 of the XLR, then connect the DIN pins 4 and 5 to the XLR pins 2 and 3. Adapters like this can enable a MIDI signal to pass through an already existing microphone patch panel—a very handy feature when trying to run the sound module (in the control room) from the keyboard (in the studio). Avoid any MIDI cable run longer than 50 feet.

MIDI Pin Numbers

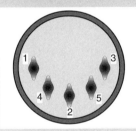

What Do MIDI Parameters Affect?
The MIDI language has been developed to control almost any part of the performance imaginable. When a key is struck, a MIDI interpretation is rendered for the note name as well as when it was struck;

how fast it was struck; when it was released; what happened with the key pressure while it was sustained; whether and how a pedal, mod wheel, or pitch control was used; the volume, pan, effects, and balance settings. There's also protocol for customizing the language for updates as well as instrument-specific instructions and commands.

The MIDI language only offers 128 steps of resolution (0–127). Therefore, if you use MIDI volume controller number 7 for a volume fade out, you don't really get an infinitely smooth fade as you would with an analog fader. What you do get is a stair-step transition through 128 MIDI values. It's not likely that you'll hear each individual step, but sometimes the MIDI parameter adjustment is audible. We refer to this audible stair-step as the zipper effect.

Controllers

Many of the MIDI parameters deal with musical expression as it would be conveyed during a live performance. MIDI instruments utilize continuous and switched controllers to control things like pitch bend, modulation, volume, and sustain. There are a total of 128 controllable parameters in MIDI spec. Controllers 0–63 are used as continuous controllers. Controllers 64–95 are used as switches. Controllers 96–121 are undefined, and 122–127 are reserved for channel mode messages.

Two or more performance wheels located to the left of the master keyboard typically vary these controller values. The performance wheels can usually be assigned to control any of the continuous controllers as well as some of the switched parameters. Aside from the performance wheels, foot pedals can also access the controllable parameters, which are also assignable to various MIDI control functions.

MIDI Controller Numbers

There are a total of 128 controllable parameters in the MIDI spec. Controllers 0–63 are used as continuous controllers. Controllers 64–95 are used as switches. Controllers 96–121 are undefined, and 122–127 are reserved for channel mode messages.

0	Bank Select	75	Undefined/Reverb
1	Modulation Wheel	76	Undefined/Delay
2	Breath Controller	77	Undefined/Pitch
3	Undefined		Transpose
4	Foot Controller	78	Undefined/Flange-Chorus
5	Portamento Time	79	Undefined/Special Effects
6	Data Entry	80–83	General Purpose 5 – 8
7	Main Volume	84	Portamento Control
8	Balance	85–90	Undefined
9	Undefined	91	Effects Depth (Effect 1)
10	Pan	92	Tremolo Depth (Effect 2)
11	Expression	93	Chorus Depth (Effect 3)
12	Effect Control 1	94	Celeste Depth (Effect 4)
13	Effect Control 2	95	Phaser Depth (Effect 5)
14	Undefined	96	Data Increment
15	Undefined	97	Data Decrement
16–19	General Purpose 1 – 4	98	Nonregistered Parameter
20–31	Undefined		Number LSB
32–63	LSB Value for	99	Nonregistered Parameter
	Controllers 0 – 31		Number MSB
64	Damper/Sustain Pedal	100	Registered Parameter
65	Portamento		Number LSB
66	Sostenuto	101	Registered Parameter
67	Soft Pedal		Number MSB
68	Legato Footswitch	102–119	Undefined
69	Hold 2	120	All Sound Off
70	Sound Variation/Exciter	121	Reset All Controllers
71	Harmonic	122	Local Control
	Content/Compressor	123	All Notes Off
72	Release Time/Distortion	124	Omni Mode Off
73	Attack Time/Equalizer	125	Omni Mode On
74	Brightness/Expander-	126	Mono Mode On
	Gate	127	Poly Mode On

Daisy Chain

If you'd like to control two separate MIDI devices with one MIDI controller, connect MIDI OUT of the controlling device to MIDI IN of the first device being controlled, then connect MIDI THRU of that device to MIDI IN of the second device being controlled. This procedure is called "daisy chaining." It isn't the best way to connect several MIDI devices together, but it is an acceptable setup if you don't connect more than a few MIDI devices to the chain.

Remember, each additional device adds approximately a three-millisecond delay to the chain. So, if you use three keyboards (one controller and two sound modules) the first module would be delayed three milliseconds and the second would be delayed six milliseconds. If you keep the instruments that need to rhythmically lock together (like drums and bass) at the very front of the daisy chain and instruments with slower attacks (like strings) at the rear of the chain, all should be well.

If you're using a computer-based sequencer, chances are the sequencer program will let you shift tracks in time. Try shifting each track in the daisy chain forward in multiples of three milliseconds, depending on which link each part is in the chain.

Listen to Audio Example 1 to hear the effect of daisy chaining. By the time the seventh slave device has received its MIDI data there's a noticeable delay. Using these percussive sounds, it's clear that there's an adverse rhythmic consequence when daisy-chaining.

Audio Example 1

Daisy Chain Delay

Daisy Chaining

Each additional device adds approximately a three-millisecond delay to the chain. If you keep the instruments that need to rhythmically lock together (like drums and bass) at the very front of the daisy chain and instruments with slower attacks (like strings) at the rear of the chain, all should be well.

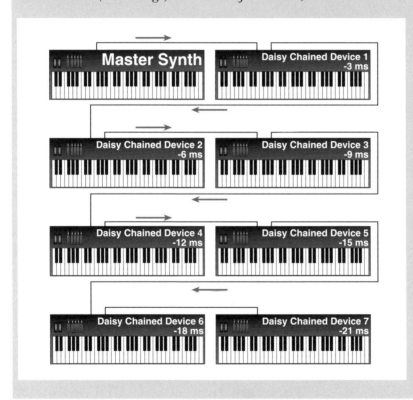

Channels

The MIDI communication language provides an option that is not only convenient, but also essential when using multiple MIDI sound sources. MIDI channels help the sound modules or synths determine which data to receive. You can send the piano, bass, drums, etc., all at once, in the same MIDI data stream. If you select MIDI channel 1 for the piano send, channel 2 for the bass, and channel 3 for the drums, you can send them, even through a daisy chain, to three separate sound modules. Simply set the piano module to receive only MIDI channel 1, the bass module to receive only MIDI channel 2, and the drum module to receive only channel 3. The modules will sift through all the MIDI data and receive only that which is tagged as belonging to its channel.

There are 16 standard MIDI channels written into the MIDI language specification; therefore, in theory, you could daisy chain up to 16 sound modules, instructing each module to receive a unique MIDI channel. In other words, you could send 16 separate musical parts—one to each module. This approach is often unacceptable because, by the time the signal reaches the end of the daisy chain, the signal has been delayed by about 45 milliseconds; that's a substantial delay.

The multicable MIDI interface is the answer to this delay problem.

MIDI Interface

Even though MIDI is a computer language, it doesn't naturally fit into the operating system of most computers. A MIDI interface is the actual hardware that transforms the MIDI language into a format that can be sent and received from a computer. Most workstations contain their own internal MIDI interface that interprets data for the built-in processor. Some computers are equipped with an internal MIDI interface, but typically the most flexible and expandable approach involves an external interface.

Some interfaces are very simple, containing one or two MIDI inputs and one or two MIDI outputs. For a small system, utilizing only a few synths or sound modules, this type of interface works very well.

With the advent of multichannel sound modules and MIDI controlled mixers and processors, the MIDI language by itself runs out of gas, quickly. It's just not practical to daisy chain everything together, and many MIDI instruments can send and receive 16 MIDI channels at once.

Instruments capable of receiving more than one MIDI channel at the same time are called multitimbral. A common setup includes several multitimbral sound modules along with MIDI controlled effects processors, a MIDI controlled mixer, and probably MIDI machine control running the multitrack.

A common setup includes several multitimbral sound modules along with MIDI controlled effects processors, and a MIDI controlled mixer with MIDI machine control running the multitrack.

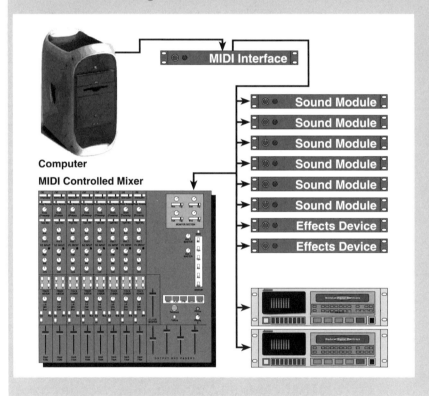

The multicable MIDI interface addresses this problem very sufficiently. Its basic operating principle is the same as the simple interface, although it processes all 16 MIDI channels through multiple cables. Most interfaces of this type offer eight separate cables that contain information for all 16 MIDI channels. This increases the power of MIDI dramatically. Not only does it multiply the available channels by the number of separate cables, but it sends all the data in perfect sync. Daisy chaining, and its time delay problems, becomes a non-issue. You could use eight multitimbral sound modules with this type of interface and gain access to 128 MIDI channels! (That's eight cables multiplied by 16 MIDI channels.)

To add to the power offered by this kind of setup, the interfaces can usually be chained together. Four of these interfaces together would let you access 512 MIDI channels, although one would have to create quite a huge MIDI setup to need 512 MIDI channels.

Multicable MIDI Interface

The multicable MIDI interface sends all 16 MIDI channels simultaneously out of eight MIDI ports. Using this type of interface, the user can access up to eight multitimbral devices with absolutely no timing discrepancies among them. To add to the power offered by this kind of setup, the interfaces can usually be linked together. Four of these interfaces together would let you access 512 MIDI channels with no timing problems!

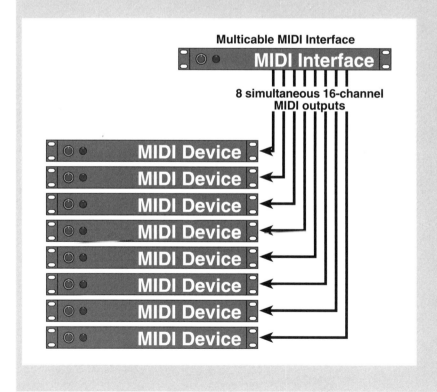

Multicable MIDI Interface

MIDI Interface

8 simultaneous 16-channel MIDI outputs

MIDI Device
MIDI Device
MIDI Device
MIDI Device
MIDI Device
MIDI Device
MIDI Device
MIDI Device

MIDI Parameters

Omni Mode

A sound module set to Omni MIDI mode hears and responds to all MIDI signals on all channels. This is not a common usage mode for song production, but it's a good mode for verifying connection between MIDI devices.

Multi Mode

Multi mode (multitimbral mode) is the most common MIDI working mode. Sound modules and synths set to multi mode discriminate between channel-specific signals. MIDI channel 1 only responds to information sent on channel 1; MIDI channel 2 only responds to information sent on channel 2; and so forth. This mode lets you develop the most individual parts from the available MIDI tools.

Mono Mode

Mono mode sets the synth to respond to just one note at a time. The original synths from Moog and Arp only had mono mode with no MIDI. They were simply single-voice oscillators with a set of filters to carve away at the sound. This subtractive form of synthesis had its own character and personality. To create a vintage musical line with a vintage synth feel, set up a fairly edgy sound in mono mode.

Mono mode is also applicable when you're driving a sound module with a guitar synthesizer, or anytime you're trying to emulate an instrument that only emits one note at a time, like a flute, clarinet, trumpet, saxophone, etc.

Polyphony versus Multitimbrality

Polyphony is simply the synth's ability to output more than one note at a time. Most modern synthesizers offer at least 32-voice polyphony; many offer 64-voice polyphony or more.

Whereas a polyphonic synth is capable of playing many notes at once, a multitimbral synth is capable of playing more than one MIDI channel at a time. Most modern synths and sound modules have 16-part multitimbrality—they can output sounds from all 16 MIDI channels at once.

Polyphonic voices are typically allocated to multitimbral MIDI channels on an as needed basis. If your sound module has 32-voice polyphony, you could theoretically use seven voices on a piano harmony part, along with eight drum and percussion tracks, a 6-voice string pad, a 4-voice guitar part, a 1-voice bass guitar track, a 1-voice melody track, and a 5-part brass section track before you ran out of voices—and that's only if all the parts were playing at once. Voice allocation uses whatever voices are available at any given moment. Your arrangement might only use 16 voices at the peak of its activity, so this type of arrangement would probably be pretty safe to perform on a 32-voice multitimbral sound module. Keep in mind, if any of the sounds you're using are layered, the

Sound Advice on MIDI

number of voices used multiplies by the number of layers.

MIDI Time Code

MIDI Time Code is the MIDI equivalent to SMPTE Time Code. MIDI language converts the hours, minutes, seconds, frames, and subframes from SMPTE into MIDI commands. MIDI Time Code (MTC) lets MIDI devices communicate via a time specific reference in much the same way a machine synchronizer communicates through SMPTE to match the time address of two mechanical drive systems.

System Messages

System Exclusive (Sys Ex)

Each manufacturer develops a communication language that's specific to its own gear. They customize their commands and develop product-specific languages for patch dumps, preset selections, editing parameters, and other special commands. All of these forms of data can be stored in a musical sequence, greatly increasing its power and flexibility. It also allows the accurate recall of sounds and adjustments that are so musically important; it's never fun to rebuild the sounds in a mix. System exclusive messages provide a means to restore the magic at a later date, with minimal discomfort.

System exclusive data consists of three parts: the header, the body, and the "end of message" byte. The header simply identifies the manufacturer specific codes; the body contains the actual data; and the end of message byte, F7, simply signifies the end of the sys ex transmission.

MIDI specification requires that system exclusive messages begin with F0 and end with F7. The body is determined by the equipment needs and the manufacturer's specifications. These messages vary in size but are always recorded as a single event by a MIDI sequencer; therefore, on particularly large sys ex messages (some can be

10–20K), the sequencer might halt playback for a second or so while the data is transmitted. This can cause a problem if you don't strategically position sys ex data transmission within the sequence. It's typically workable to place sys ex transmissions at the beginning of the sequence, separated from the first MIDI note by a measure or so, depending on the amount of information that needs to be transferred. If the setup for a sequence requires a lot of system exclusive data, it's a good idea to place the sys ex data in a separate setup sequence.

A system exclusive message looks like a single line in most sequencing software packages. In reality, they are typically fairly large hexadecimal files. This data can usually be edited, but be sure to do your homework on the product before you start tweaking a system exclusive message—you could cause more problems than you solve.

System Exclusive Messages

A system exclusive message looks like a single line in most sequencing software packages. In reality, they are typically fairly large hexadecimal files. This data can usually be edited, but be sure to do your homework on the product before you start tweaking a system exclusive message—you could cause more problems than you solve.

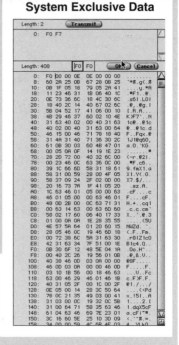

System Exclusive Data

System Exclusive Message

Data Dump

A MIDI data dump is merely a MIDI data transmission, either from the MIDI device to a sequencer or from a sequencer back to the device. Some manufacturers have set a product-specific specification that transmits system messages on only one channel; but, as a rule, system exclusive messages typically have no channel assignment. So, if you're daisy chaining synths together, all synths and sound modules connected together to a single MIDI output will receive the entire sys ex dump. This usually isn't a problem if all the modules and synths are made by separate manufacturers because they shouldn't recognize each other's specific data. If you have two or three synths from the same manufacturer connected in a daisy chain to one MIDI out port, they'll all receive the sys ex information—no matter what MIDI channel they're assigned to! If you don't want them all set exactly the same, this is a big problem. An error in system exclusive transmission could wipe out the programs, layers, presets, and multitimbral combinations in one or more of your sound modules!

The multicable MIDI interface helps this problem because information can sent through only one cable to a single module, with no daisy chaining involved. With this kind of setup, there shouldn't be any problem transmitting sys ex information because the data is only sent to the module on the assigned MIDI port.

If you have a large daisy chain set up, you might need to connect your modules, one at a time, for a system exclusive data dump, reconnecting the daisy chain only when all units' system exclusive transmissions have completed.

The Handshake

Some MIDI devices require a specific handshake message before they'll play, receive, or dump any data stream. If you experience a problem with transmitting and receiving sys ex messages, consult the manual for the device; if your piece of gear requires a handshake message, that message will most likely be noted in the chapter on system exclusive.

If you're using a computer-based sequencer, you can usually simply enter the handshake message in a system exclusive sequence. Once it's entered and can be transmitted, everything should work well. Keep in mind that the handshake will probably need to be sent to the device before the device will dump to the sequencer. It will also need to be transmitted before the sequencer can dump into the device.

Data Backup

Since system exclusive data transmissions have the potential to wipe out your synth, sound module, processor, or mixer settings, it is a very good idea to always keep a backup of your important system exclusive data for each MIDI instrument. It's a fairly simple procedure to create a system exclusive archival sequence for each MIDI instrument. Name and date the sequence. If applicable, include a reference to the song title in the sequence name. Do whatever it takes to eliminate the guesswork when you need to restore your MIDI gear to a previous configuration.

If, by chance, you transmit a spurious system exclusive message and one of your MIDI devices locks up or seems to have lost its data, try turning the unit off and then back on again before you break out your backup system sequences. Many devices recall their settings when powered up—or there might be a key combination that restores default settings on power up.

General MIDI Specifications

Manufacturers agreed in 1991 to a specific set of MIDI standards called General MIDI (GM). GM standardizes locations and MIDI channels for synths and sound modules, allowing musicians to share sequencing work with some assurance that their sequence can be easily played back.

GM synthesizers support all 16 MIDI channels and offer at least 24-voice polyphony and 16-voice multitimbral output, for a minimum of one voice available for each MIDI channel. Percussion parts are always on MIDI channel 10, using a minimum set of 47 standard drum and percussion sounds, mapped according to the GM standard.

All 128 program sounds are defined as to their type and patch location. Even

General MIDI Drum Sound Map

MIDI Note #	GM Drum Sound	MIDI Note #	GM Drum Sound	MIDI Note #	GM Drum Sound
35	Acoustic Bass Drum	50	High Tom	66	Low Timbale
		51	Ride Cymbal	67	High Agogo
36	Bass Drum 1	52	Chinese Cymbal	68	Low Agogo
37	Side Stick	53	Ride Bell	69	Cabasa
38	Acoustic Snare	54	Tambourine	70	Maracas
39	Hand Clap	55	Splash Cymbal	71	Short Whistle
40	Electric Snare	56	Cowbell	72	Long Whistle
41	Low Floor Tom	57	Crash Cymbal 2	73	Short Guiro
42	Closed Hi-hat	58	Vibraslap	74	Long Guiro
43	High Floor Tom	59	Ride Cybmal 2	75	Claves
44	Pedal Hi-hat	60	High Bongo	76	High Woodblock
45	Low Tom	61	Low Bongo	77	Low Woodblock
46	Open Hi-hat	62	Mute High Conga	78	Mute Cuica
47	Low Mid Tom	63	Open High Conga	79	Open Cuica
48	High Mid Tom	64	Low Conga	80	Mute Trinagle
49	Crash Cymbal	65	High Timbale	81	Open Triangle

though sound modules vary substantially in their sound quality and subjective appeal, the General MIDI standard is still very effective in its ability to coordinate an otherwise disjunct and separated segment of the music industry. It's very convenient for publishers and songwriters to distribute MIDI files with some assurance that they'll make musical sense on playback. It provides a means to share or sell MIDI tracks that can be edited and customized by the recipient.

General MIDI devices all respond to the same set of controllers, with predetermined and standardized ranges for each. GM devices need to respond, in like manner, to pitch bend, velocity, aftertouch, master tuning, reset all controllers, and all notes off commands.

GM2, the second generation General MIDI specification, extends the protocol to include more parameters than GM1. The addition of most of the effects controllers and more note data parameters provide more potential and flexibility in this MIDI standard.

General MIDI Voices

Program Number	GM Voice	Program Number	GM Voice	Program Number	GM Voice
1	Acoustic Grand	44	Contrabass	87	Lead 7 (Fifths)
2	Bright Acoustic Piano	45	Tremelo Strings	88	Lead 8 (Bass + Lead)
3	Electric Grand Piano	46	Pizzicato Strings	89	Pad 1 (New Age)
4	Honky-Tonk Piano	47	Orchestral Harp	90	Pad 2 (Warm)
5	Electric Piano 1	48	Timpani	91	Pad 3 (Polysynth)
6	Electric Piano 2	49	String Ensemble 1	92	Pad 4 (Choir)
7	Harpsichord	50	String Ensemble 2	93	Pad 5 (Bowed)
8	Clavinet	51	SynthStrings 1	94	Pad 6 (Metallic)
9	Celesta	52	SynthStrings 2	95	Pad 7 (Halo)
10	Glockenspiel	53	Choir Aahs	96	Pad 8 (Sweep)
11	Music Box	54	Voice Oohs	97	FX 1 (Rain)
12	Vibraphone	55	Synth Voice	98	FX 2 (Soundtrack)
13	Marimba	56	Orchestra Hits	99	FX 3 (Crystal)
14	Xylophone	57	Trumpet	100	FX 4 (Atmosphere)
15	Tubular Bells	58	Trombone	101	FX 5 (Brightness)
16	Dulcimer	59	Tuba	102	FX 6 (Goblins)
17	Drawbar Organ	60	Muted Trumpet	103	FX 7 (Echoes)
18	Percussive Organ	61	French Horn	104	FX 8 (Sci-Fi)
19	Rock Organ	62	Brass Section	105	Sitar
20	Church Organ	63	SynthBrass 1	106	Banjo
21	Reed Organ	64	SynthBrass 2	107	Shamisen
22	Accordian	65	Soprano Sax	108	Koto
23	Harmonica	66	Alto Sax	109	Kalimba
24	Tango Accordian	67	Tenor Sax	110	Bagpipe
25	Acoustic Guitar (Nylon)	68	Baritone Sax	111	Fiddle
26	Acoustic Guitar (Steel)	69	Oboe	112	Shanai
27	Electric Guitar (Jazz)	70	English Horn	113	Tinkle Bell
28	Electric Guitar (Clean)	71	Bassoon	114	Agogo
29	Electric Guitar (Muted)	72	Clarinet	115	Steel Drum
30	Overdriven Guitar	73	Piccolo	116	Woodblock
31	Distortion Guitar	74	Flute	117	Taiko Drum
32	Guitar Harmonics	75	Recorder	118	Melodic Tom
33	Acoustic Bass	76	Pan Flute	119	Synth Drum
34	Electric Bass (Finger)	77	Blown Bottle	120	Reverse Cymbal
35	Electric Bass (Pick)	78	Shakuhachi	121	Guitar Fret Noise
36	Fretless Bass	79	Whistle	122	Breath Noise
37	Slap Bass 1	80	Ocarina	123	Seashore
38	Slap Bass 2	81	Lead 1 (Square)	124	Bird Tweet
39	Synth Bass 1	82	Lead 2 (Sawtooth)	125	Telephone Ring
40	Synth Bass 2	83	Lead 3 (Calliope)	126	Helicopter
41	Violin	84	Lead 4 (Chiff)	127	Applause
42	Viola	85	Lead 5 (Charang)	128	Gunshot
43	Cello	86	Lead 6 (Voice)		

MIDI Machine Control (MMC)

MIDI Machine Control uses specific MIDI commands for controlling transport and cueing functions. Most modern recorders like those made by Alesis, Tascam, Sony, Fostex, Otari, etc. can be controlled through MMC. These machines must be connected, through standard MIDI cables and an interface, to the MIDI controller. The specific controller could be a software-based sequencing/digital audio package, a dedicated hardware controller, or a master tape machine.

Whether hardware- or software-based, MMC controls look and act like tape-deck style transport controls. In a typical setup, the MMC controller sends transport commands to another MMC device, which serves as an address master. The address master generates and distributes time code information to all recording and playback devices, which, in turn, chase and lock according to the MMC commands.

It's not necessary that post-address master devices and machines respond to MMC commands; they must simply follow the timing commands supplied by the address master.

MIDI Machine Control

MIDI Machine Control is a very convenient means of controlling physical transports from within your computer-based digital recording system. The screen below controls multiple machines while the MIDI sequence plays along. All sequence transport and record commands are functional for the connected tape machines as well.

Synchronization

Synchronizing recording equipment is similar to synchronizing musicians and swimmers:

- It's ideal if all gear is in exactly the same groove. It's easier to get everyone working together if all participants speak the same language.

- Some players, swimmers, and recording equipment are better at synchronizing accurately than others.

- Every once in a while, even the best have a bad day and, for unexplained reasons, mess up everybody that they're around.

Now we'll cover some different types of synchronization and how they might or might not work well together. Our goal is to understand all the ingredients in order to make informed and insightful decisions regarding system configurations and equipment purchase options.

Synchronizing Basics

Any synchronization system needs a master transport, which all others follow. Devices that follow the master are called slaves, and they must follow the master within the tightest sync tolerance possible. Different types of synchronization schemes offer varying degrees of accuracy. Some systems are relatively loose, with machines fading back and forth in relation to the master speed. Other, newer systems are able to remain locked to sample-accurate perfection. In a sample-accurate synchronization system, the machines are locked so tightly together that they act like one. If the master machine plays back at a sample rate of 48kHz, so does the slave. The slave verifies at each sample that it's still in sync, and it doesn't drift at all.

In its infancy, the synchronization process was primal compared to our current capabilities. Early schemes, like pilot tone, were an attempt to control film transports so that audio and film images could be combined after the final film print was completed. As the film and television industries grew, SMPTE became an industry standard for synchronizing image to picture; it provided much more flexibility. The simple ability to start, stop, and resume playback at any point in a program while maintaining sync between all SMPTE-savvy machines was a boon. With modern synchronization methods and protocol, not only can many machines sync quickly and easily, but they can sync in a sample accurate manner. Modern systems can synchronize many devices, representing hundreds of audio tracks, together so that they act and sound like a single machine.

Why Bother?

This question has become increasingly valid with the advent of powerful new digital audio/MIDI sequencing software packages. If you have a huge hard drive and you record only within your computer domain, you probably haven't needed to worry too much about synchronizing concerns yet. If you simply bounce your mixes to disk, then save them to CD or DVD, you're probably still immune to the sync plague. But, if you need to record your mixes to DAT, if you're jumping into the digital mixer world, if you want to get the most out of your outboard digital effects, if you ever plan on interconnecting to the professional world, or if you think your music has any chance whatsoever to make it to the next level of industry greatness, you're going to need to address synchronization in a serious way.

MIDI to Audio Sync

MIDI to audio sync has made great strides in the area of convenience. Compared to manual sync, pilot tone, sync pulse, song position pointer, and FSK, the SMPTE based system (often referred to as LTC [Longitudinal Time Code]) is fast, accurate,

and fairly simple to master. SMPTE/MTC
offers compatibility across the industry
and serves us well in many cases.

Timing Discrepancies

MTC and SMPTE are good standards, but
they're definitely not precisely accurate.
The SMPTE to MTC translation is slow.
It's dependent on the integrity and quality
of the time SMPTE code. It often has to
interpret what it thinks the time code
should have been, and it's not always right.

Devices syncing to SMPTE/MTC float
back and forth in time depending on a
several factors:

- Is the data transfer to and from the
  MIDI device going through a bottle-
  neck, or can it flow freely and
  uninhibited?

- Is the device's processor fast enough to
  keep up with the demand of the MIDI
  sequence data?

- Is there digital audio data competing for the internal clock or computer processor power?

- Is the MIDI interface keeping up with the demand for multichannel data transfer?

- Is the master MIDI device running from its internal clock, or is it chasing another SMPTE-based device?

- Is there a grand master system clock acting as the time base for the complete system? If so, what kind of timing clock is it?

Many recordists feel that the SMPTE/ MTC synchronization system is a perfect synchronization environment. It's not. The best accuracy factor we can hope for whenever using a SMPTE/MTC based master is ±1/4 frame. That might not seem unreasonable at first glance, but if we calculate the delay, we soon recognize a significant sync variance. If we assume a frame rate of 30 frames per second, it's easy to calculate that, since each frame occupies 1/30 of the 1000ms in a single second, a single frame is about 33 1/3ms. Each quarter frame is about 8 1/3ms. A variance of ±1/4 provides a net error of up to 16 2/3ms, and that's touted to be about as good as it gets.

This degree of error is not too disturbing until you begin to combine devices, transfer data, and interconnect various systems over the course of time. With a ±8 1/3ms error factor, the recordist can't be certain that every pass of every take in every generation will respond to synchronization in exactly the same manner. It's possible for the margin of error to compound over the course of a project, especially whenever combining recording formats and sync devices. The quarter frame error factor can multiply throughout the life of a project, resulting in a musical feel that is much different from the one you slaved to create in the beginning.

Audio Example 2 demonstrates the rhythmic effect of the error factor in MTC and how it can compound over the life of a project.

Audio Example 2
Panned Clicks Simulating MTC Error Factor

Audio example 3 through 5 demonstrate the sound of a drum track rushed and laid back by the potential margin of error in the MTC-based system.

Audio Example 3
Original Drum Part

Audio Example 4
Drum Part Delayed by 33 1/3 ms

Audio Example 5
Drum Part Moved Ahead by 33 1/3 ms

There is no solution to this lack of accuracy as long as the master clock device is SMPTE/MTC based.

MIDI to MIDI Sync

MIDI to MIDI synchronization is a reasonably simple process. MIDI Time Code (MTC) is simply transmitted through the MIDI cable connecting the synchronized device. Modern MIDI devices include an option to sync to an external source. Once that option is selected, it waits to receive MTC, then plays along in near perfect time.

MTC is a very common time communication format. Many digital devices and recorders synchronize according to MTC language. MTC is the MIDI equivalent of SMPTE time code, referenced to hours, minutes, seconds, frames, and subframes.

Accuracy

The accuracy factor of MTC in the MIDI to MIDI communication domain is much more solid than SMPTE-based audio to MIDI sync. An accuracy factor of ±1 tick can be expected in most cases (a tick is typically 1/480 of a beat). Therefore, the accuracy is dependent on the tempo of the song. At 120 quarter notes per minute, we can expect accuracy to within ±1.04ms (500ms/beat÷480 ticks).

MTC Connections

Most software packages provide a way to send MTC and other synchronizing information to any machine or MIDI device in the system. Simply drag from one device to another to connect them through the digital, on-screen patching system.

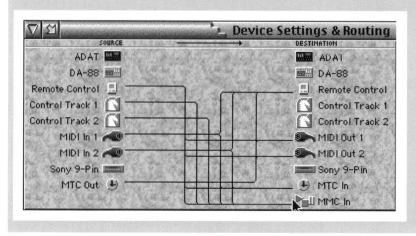

Accuracy in MIDI to MIDI sync (MTC to MTC) is still dependent on data bottlenecks, processor speed, time clock source, etc..

Logjam

If a MIDI transmission contains a lot of controller motion, like pitch bend or modulation, the bulk of data can cause a MIDI logjam. As all the data flows at once, sometimes it gets stuck, causing what sounds like a timing hiccup. The short pause, as the data regains its flow, renders the particular playback useless.

The logjam can be eliminated in a couple different ways. First, consider purchasing an interface with a higher data transfer rate. This solution can save you a lot of heartache later. Second, look for an option that lets you thin the controller data. This command might be called Thin Continuous Data or Thin Controller Data, or some similar rendition. This command eliminates a percentage of the data. If you set the command to 50 percent, it will remove every other controller command, dramatically decreasing the bulk of the data. Most of the time, thinning data has no real effect on the sound of the performance, and it usually eliminates the MIDI logjam.

Offsets

Offsets provide a means to adjust timing between machines. If you come across two reels of tape, or devices, that must be synchronized, the time code references on each might not exactly match the other. In this case, the proper difference between the two time code positions must be guessed, then finely adjusted until the devices or machines work together in an efficient and musical way.

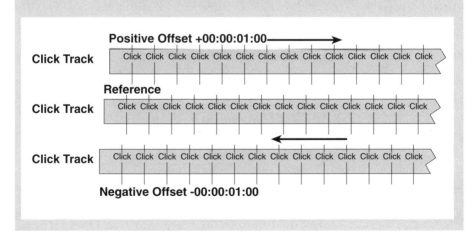

Regenerating Time Code

Time code that comes from a tape track often loses its precise definition in the recording process. Sometimes bits of code will be lost or damaged. Therefore, it's advisable to regenerate time code anytime it must be recorded from one tape track to another. It's a good idea to regenerate the code even when it's coming from a tape track into a computer-based system.

The generator simultaneously outputs the exact code it receives at its input. In fact, it compensates for minor dropouts in the incoming code which might have been caused by tape anomalies or wear.

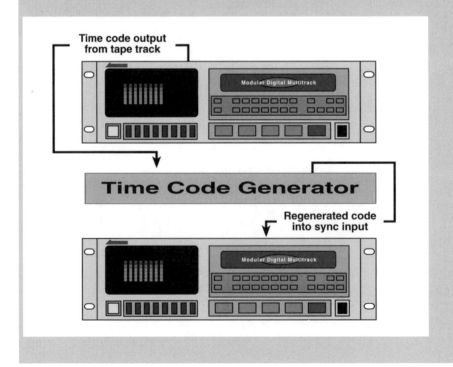

Processor Speed

Processor speed is very important, especially when using a digital combined audio/MIDI sequencing software package. It's likely that a large file with a substantial amount of digital audio will occupy the processor to such an extent that the timing clock bogs down. With this, the tempo and time feel go up in smoke. The solution to this type of problem is to either buy a faster, bigger, meaner computer; thin out your files so there aren't any unnecessary competitors lurking in the wings; or turn all nonessential system extensions off.

Standard MIDI File

Cross-Platform Compatibility

With so many types of sequencers and software packages available for MIDI sequencing, the MIDI music industry made a mature decision a number of years ago to create a standardized format that could be read by any MIDI sequencer. Sometimes track names or other visual formats are lost in the translation, but, at the very least, all notes and control parameters remain intact whenever a standard MIDI file is saved from one sequencer and then opened in another.

The standard MIDI file is an excellent transition format between your MIDI sequencer and notation software. It's typical to record a sequence in the sequencer software first, in order to determine the arrangement and orchestration, and to later save a copy in standard MIDI file format. The standard MIDI file then opens up splendidly from your music notation software, where the lyrics and print refinements are added to create a professional looking piece of music.

There are also very useful applications for beginning your song in the notation package. This approach lets you refine any instrumental arrangements and orchestrations, transferring them through the standard MIDI file to the sequencer once they're perfected. Files that are begun in notation package are typically quantized to 100 percent, so you might need to use the available sequencer functions to randomize, humanize, and generally spruce up the sequence.

Strings and Pads

Layering

When you hear a string pad that sounds rich, full and very interesting, the appeal isn't always the result of an incredible raw sound. What's been done with the sound is often the most impressive part. One technique that consistently produces good interesting sounds is layering. Layering is a common keyboard term that refers to the process of stacking one sound on top of another. Within the keyboard, layering is done by assigning two or more internal sounds to play at once, every time you hit a key. This works so well because, as the two basic sounds interact, the harmonics and overtones combine. Rather than continually shaping one sound to achieve just the right sound, find two separate sounds that each contain part of what you need, then play them together.

One of the ways we can create interesting new sounds that no one has heard before is by layering one keyboard with a different keyboard. The chances of someone creating the exact sound that you've found, combining a Triton with an QS-8, for instance, aren't nearly as likely as if you'd layered two of the standard internal QS-8 sounds. Take advantage of the tools that are available to you. Just because a keyboard isn't the newest piece of technology on the block doesn't mean that it won't sound great with another keyboard or sound module.

Listen to the two fairly plain and simple string sounds in Audio Example 6. I'll play the parts separately, then I'll layer them together. Notice how they take on a much more rich and interesting character when they're heard together than when they're heard separately.

Audio Example 6
Layering

If there are enough tracks or channels available, pan the two keyboards slightly apart to simulate a wider "section" sound, as in Audio Example 7.

Audio Example 7
Panning the Layered Sounds Apart

A common technique when layering sounds is to slightly de-tune the sounds. This accentuates the harmonic interaction between the two sounds, creating a larger overall feel. This technique has the potential to be extreme, since we're layering two different sounds rather than simply running one sound through the harmonizer.

In Audio Example 8, I'll slightly de-tune the two different string sounds. One keyboard is tuned eight cents sharp and the other is tuned eight cents flat. If your keyboard doesn't have a tuner that indicates tuning by cents, try using a guitar tuner; most guitar tuners show tuning in cents. I'll add these sounds one at a time, pan them apart, then pan them together to center.

Audio Example 8
De-tuning Two String Sounds

The technique of layering can be carried as far as your mixer, tracks and available keyboards will allow. Although you can reach a point where simply adding one more keyboard sound doesn't make much of a difference, it is common to use two, three or even four keyboards playing the identical part to shape an interesting, unique sound.

Use each keyboard or sound module for a specific part of the overall sound you're building. Samplers often help to add realism. If a very intimate sampled string sound—including the sound of the bow scraping across the strings—is combined with a very full lush pad, the result is usually very impressive and full.

In Audio Example 9, I'll combine three elements: the bright sampled single-string sound, the large defined string pad and the mellow, filling, smooth string pad. I'll play each sound separately, then combine them; finally, I'll vary their pan placement. Notice how the sum of all these parts sounds much better—and more interesting—than any of the individual pieces.

Audio Example 9
Layering Three Sounds

Quantizing

The Basics

Quantizing cleans up inaccuracies in a musical performance. For the purposes of this section, we're considering the quantizing of musical notes, but many sequencers offer the ability to quantize many different MIDI parameters.

In the process of quantizing, each note or parameter is viewed by the sequencer in relation to a note-value grid. The user specifies whether the grid references quarter notes, sixteenth notes, eighth note triplets, etc. Each note of the performance is pulled to the closest grid unit. If you play a note just after the third sixteenth note of count three, and your grid is set to sixteenth notes, the sequencer will pull the note exactly to the mathematically correct third sixteenth note of beat three. If you perform a note between two grid units, the sequencer will pull the note onto the closest grid unit; so, if the performance is too sloppy, the sequencer might pull some notes to the wrong beats.

Early model sequencers popularized the concept of quantizing, sometimes called auto-correct. The idea that you could play rhythmically sloppy parts, then have a box make your performance rhythmically perfect was a big hit. The only problem is that nobody really plays rhythmically perfect every time, so the sequencer was soon labeled as mechanical sounding, or machinelike. Since everything was quantized to perfection, there was no emotional personalization.

Technology has given us nearly complete control over musical performances. Nowadays, the recordist can be blamed as much for a sloppy performance as the artist. However, even with the nearly complete control available in recording, it's important to understand that recording decisions must be based on musical grounds, not on binary hexadecimal codes. We can however, tighten a performance to within specified tolerances and if it's too tight we can randomize to whatever degree we choose.

Quantizing

The process of quantizing pulls each note of a performance to the closest background unit. If you've set the sequencer to quantize to the closest eighth note (like the example below) each note will be drawn to the closest eighth note. Notice the inaccuracy of the beat placements in Example 1—hardly any notes fall directly on the beat. Example 2 has been quantized; notice how each note is perfectly placed on the eighth note grid.

Be careful. If you perform a note between two grid units, the sequencer will pull the note onto the closest grid unit; so, if the performance is too sloppy, the sequencer might pull some notes to the wrong beats.

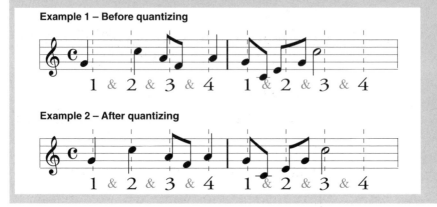

Example 1 – Before quantizing

Example 2 – After quantizing

Velocities, Durations, and Tempos

Velocities, durations, tempos, and many other musical aspects are completely controllable and moldable through MIDI manipulation. Each sequencer handles adjustments of these parameters in its own way, but the concepts are typically identical. Once you begin to understand the basics of these controls, the details fall painlessly into place. You should be able to cross between hardware and software sequencers with a minimal amount of adjustment, primarily because you'll know what to expect—you'll know what to look for.

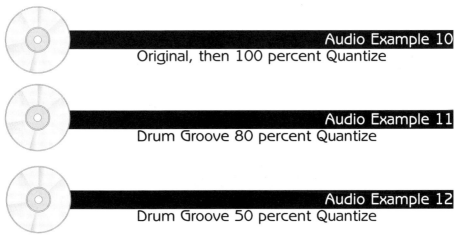

Audio Example 10
Original, then 100 percent Quantize

Audio Example 11
Drum Groove 80 percent Quantize

Audio Example 12
Drum Groove 50 percent Quantize

Quantize Percentage

Strength is a quantize parameter that determines the degree of perfection attained. Imagine a magnet, pulling the MIDI notes toward the grid. At 100 percent strength the magnet pulls the notes all the way to the grid. At 80 percent strength, the magnetic only pulls the notes 80 percent of the way toward the grid. Using the strength option is an excellent way to tighten up a musical performance without sterilizing it.

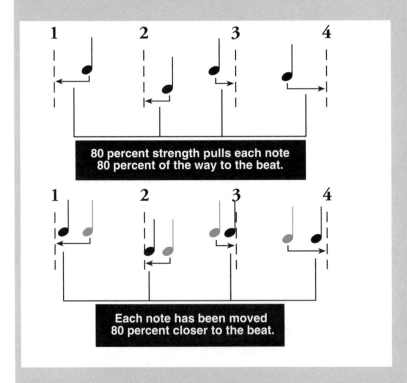

80 percent strength pulls each note 80 percent of the way to the beat.

Each note has been moved 80 percent closer to the beat.

Quantize Sensitivity

At 50 percent sensitivity, the notes in the middle 50 percent between grid locations would not be quantized, while the notes in the area extending 25 percent on either side of the grid would be quantized. Negative numbers tell the processor to quantize in relation to the center point between grid locations. So, a −50 percent sensitivity leaves the notes that surround the grid (25 percent on either side) alone, while quantizing the notes that surround the center point between grid location.

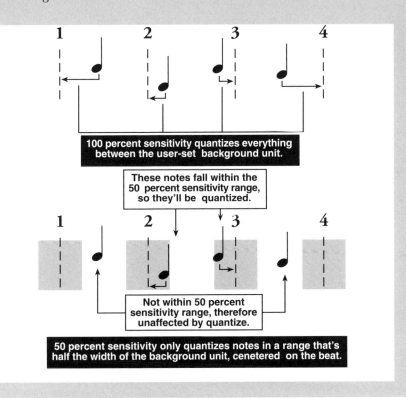

1   2   3   4

100 percent sensitivity quantizes everything between the user-set background unit.

These notes fall within the 50 percent sensitivity range, so they'll be quantized.

1   2   3   4

Not within 50 percent sensitivity range, therefore unaffected by quantize.

50 percent sensitivity only quantizes notes in a range that's half the width of the background unit, cenetered on the beat.

Absolute versus Partial Quantizing

The primary problem with 100 percent quantizing lies in the hiding of notes. If all notes are lined up perfectly on the beat, the brain doesn't have time to recognize the individual ingredients. Once the parts are spread out in a more realistic way, it's amazing how much more fun the sequence is to listen to.

Notice in the top example notice how the notes lay on top of each other. The instruments are all fighting for visibility. In the bottom example each note is more realistically spread out around the beat and is, therefore, much easier to hear and recognize. This simple concept explains why sequences often sound sterile, lacking personality and impact.

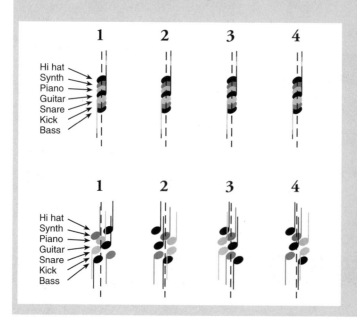

Combining MIDI Mix Tools

Amazing power comes from the combination of a digital recording/sequencing package and a digital recording console. If you throw in a modular digital multi-track—or two or three—you're in techno heaven. Prices on this gear have dropped dramatically in the past years. Because of technological advances, recoupment of development costs, and good old-fashioned competition, we can all at least have a shot at owning many of these tools. In many ways, I can do more at my home studio now than I could at any studio in the world not too long ago! The one thing most of us can't replace at home, however, is well-designed space. Professional studios offer recording environments that are full of excitement and inspiration. All you need to do is clap your hands once in a large, impeccably put together studio, and you immediately understand. Synthetic reverberation can't replace the open sound of a recording in an excellent studio.

MIDI System Design:

What Should I Have?

Let's review some MIDI abilities, capabilities, and musical applications while we map out a potential MIDI system.

Synths

- **Controller**—It's necessary to have a master keyboard to access and perform the myriad of sounds available in the MIDI world.

- **Sound Module**—Once you've chosen a master controller, it's fun, easy, and inexpensive to add sound modules. Every good synth comes in a rack-mountable version at a significantly reduced price. If you already have a sequencer and a controller, you can often save 50 percent off the keyboard/workstation by simply purchasing the module. It's easier to keep up with current sounds when you only need the scaled down sound module.

Sequencers

- **Hardware Black Boxes**—Some hardware sequencers that are sold as freestanding units offer many professional features. They're usually cheaper than the cost of a computer and a software package (especially if you include the cost of a good multi-cable MIDI interface), and they require no computer. However, they're more cumbersome, confusing, and time consuming to operate. Black boxes are appealing because they're typically designed from the ground up with accurate sequence timing in mind. They don't share a processor with any other computer function. They're often the most constant, in reference to the groove.

- **Computer Software Packages**—If it's at all financially possible, buy a computer and the best software package available. Almost everyone already has the computer, but even if you need to purchase one, this route will probably be much less expensive in the long run. Most users soon feel the frustration of a hardware sequencer (with one or two small access windows and a maze of pages to scroll through). It's often difficult to perform even basic MIDI functions with these hardware-based systems. These boxes are often sold for a fraction of what they originally cost in order to get into a computer-based system.

When it comes time to buy, check out catalogs and music stores. You'll soon find what's hot and what's not. Consider that, although the prices through mail order might be cheaper (and you might be able to dodge taxation), there'll be a time when you need help, and quickly. At

Sound Advice on MIDI

those times, you'll certainly appreciate the concept of a local, friendly, knowledgeable, helpful sales person, willing to give you on-the-spot support. If you're talking to a dealer who seems to have little or no knowledge of the product, buy elsewhere.

Interfaces

- **Simple Interface**—If you have a small MIDI setup and you don't expect it to grow much, buy an inexpensive interface.

- **Multicable**—If you have several sound modules and see growth in your future, don't waste time or money on anything other than a good multicable interface that reads and writes time code, with provision for further expansion.

Mix Controller

In the digital recording arena, although all options can be controlled onscreen within the computer or hardware, there's still a place for actually controlling the signal with a physical knob, fader, or button. Several companies offer hardware control surfaces for interfacing with some amazing software packages.

Mixers

- **Digital**—Digital mixers have become very affordable and offer tons of features, plus total automation. You can't go too far off base in this arena. But it's always important to test the mixer before you buy. The sound quality on digital mixers is usually good, but some have a grainy kind of a zing-like sound. As with any audio equipment, always listen before you buy. A manufacturer can tout features and sound quality till the cows come home, but we should all make a stand to base our purchasing decisions on sound quality, ease of use, and musicality. We are, after all, dealing with music first and technology second.

- **Analog Mixers with MIDI Control—** Most modern analog mixers offer, at the very least, MIDI controlled mutes. There's usually a set of MIDI ports on the console; just plug into your MIDI network, open the manual, and start amazing yourself with the possibilities for creative freedom.

- **MIDI Controlled Automation—**There are several MIDI controlled automation systems available. They typically have external hardware that intercepts all mixer outputs, inserting a VCA in each channel that allows for automated fader and mute control. These packages are very powerful aids in the mixing process, but they don't offer the complete control offered by a fully digital mixer.

Digital Audio Cards
Combining MIDI Sequencing and Digital Audio—If you're using a computer-based sequencer, I'd highly recommend

upgrading to a combined MIDI/digital audio package. You might or might not need to add an audio card to your computer, depending on your format and needs. The power and flexibility of housing your MIDI sequence and live audio recording in the same box is incredible. You can cut, paste, copy, and undo all audio segments in the same manner as MIDI data, and everything is on one screen. Mixing digital audio and MIDI instruments is all done on the same computer screen. It's the best way to work that I've found so far and, when run in tandem with a digital mixer, it offers phenomenal creative freedom.

Tactile Control Surfaces for Computer-Based Digital Workstations

If you have everything happening on your computer and you're frustrated by constantly reaching for the mouse and clicking on small pictures of knobs and faders, check out the newest tactile controllers on the block. For not too much cash, you can work on a manual control surface that feels like a mixer but accesses the full power of the digital and MIDI domain. It brings the comfort of an analog mixer into the bliss of digital flexibility.

Be sure the control surface manufacturer offers expansion options. If you like having 8 channels of faders, buttons, and knobs, you might really like having 16, 32, or more.

Combining MIDI and Live Recording

With the development of digital recording software that also sequences MIDI data, home recording has changed radically. I'm really a drummer who has played a lot of guitar and bass, so I've been forced to grow in my keyboard skills to even sequence the most basic synth and piano parts. In the years since MIDI software became available, I've sequenced the piano and rhythm tracks for several albums and other commercial projects.

I've been able to get by, but once I was given the tools to record my guitar parts right along with the sequenced tracks, life changed for me. Plus, I could lay down vocals and percussion and anything else I wanted. It was like a musical revival all over again. Even though I had the tools to sync my multitrack to my computer, the control and flexibility offered by the complete digital/MIDI software was amazing.

Music is changing all the time. The exciting thing about the phenomenal growth of technology is the creative freedom it provides. Most musicians feel more relaxed and emotionally free when they're at home than when they're in the studio performing under the pressure of the record light, the producer, or the clock.

Sometimes the realization of the hourly rate stifles the creative flow. Only the most seasoned studio musicians come alive in the studio environment—and then somebody else is probably paying for

the time anyway. The creative environment in the home studio should release
and increase the depth of modern music.
We all benefit.

Depending on the musical style, it's
common to record real guitar, grand
piano, vocals, and solo instruments over a
basic MIDI sequence that includes drums,
percussion, bass, and synths. Sometimes,
simply adding a sax or guitar solo over a
well produced sequence brings new life
to the whole project. With the ease of
integration between MIDI and digital
recording, we hear any combination of
recording processes all the time. In this
era, we can pick and choose the techniques
and instruments that work best for the
music, easily combining them all at home.
We might be limited by access to proficient
musicians to play the parts we need, but
the recording tools aren't the problem
anymore.

Conclusion

This book is full of MIDI facts and figures. The trick for you is to put MIDI to work in a musical way. The power of the MIDI protocol has become its flexibilty and ease of use.

Look at MIDI through creative eyes. It offers simplicity to a fault in its basic functionality. However, vast capacity is built in to go crazy. Current MIDI/Audio production software is amazing. Integration of audio tracks with MIDI functionality has opened a new door to creative options. Walk on the wild side. We'd all love to be inspired by your new and impressive use of modern technology.

InstantPro series

Take Your Recordings to the Next Level with These 6 New Titles!

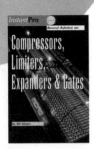

SOUND ADVICE ON COMPRESSORS, LIMITERS, EXPANDERS & GATES
Bill Gibson

When used correctly, compressors, limiters, gates, expanders and other dynamics processors are essential tools for creating recordings that sound impressive and professional. This information-packed book provides step-by-step instruction along with several excellent audio examples, all aimed at showing you how to use these important tools like a pro.
©2002, softcover with CD, $14.95
ISBN #1-931140-24-3

SOUND ADVICE ON EQUALIZERS, REVERBS & DELAYS
Bill Gibson

If you want to produce recordings that sound impressive and musical, you need this book and CD! They're filled with techniques and examples designed to help your mixes come alive. Follow step-by-step equalization guidelines for recording and mixing all popular instruments. Learn how to use reverbs and delays to set your music in a controlled, blended, and dimensional space.
©2002, softcover with CD, $14.95
ISBN #1-931140-25-1

SOUND ADVICE ON DEVELOPING YOUR HOME STUDIO
Bill Gibson

Get the most out of your home studio with this book and CD! What's the proper way to set up your gear? Does it make a difference which kind of cable you use? Will the gear you have work with the new gear you want? Where should monitors go? Should you worry about acoustics? This book has easy-to-understand answers to these questions and many more.
©2002, softcover with CD, $14.95
ISBN #1-931140-26-X

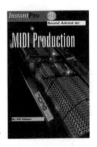

SOUND ADVICE ON MICROPHONE TECHNIQUES
Bill Gibson

Professional-sounding recordings start with a great sound source, informed microphone selection and excellent technique. Learn how the three most common microphone designs work and how to use them. Discover which microphones are recommended for different instruments and voices, and hear why on the accompanying audio CD.
©2002, softcover with CD, $14.95
ISBN #1-931140-27-8

SOUND ADVICE ON MIXING
Bill Gibson

If you want your mixes to sound great, even next to your favorite commercial release of your favorite artist, you need this book and CD! You'll learn mixing techniques and hear audio examples designed to help you create a professional-sounding mix. Avoid the pitfalls of mixing. Build a mix from the ground up, shaping each ingredient with the big picture in mind. Learn how to set up a mix that has power and impact.
©2002, softcover with CD, $14.95
1-931140-29-4

SOUND ADVICE ON MIDI PRODUCTION
Bill Gibson

Whether you're creating a MIDI sequencing extravaganza, supporting an acoustic recording, or synchronizing equipment, MIDI is likely to be involved. This book and CD will help you unlock the immense power of this essential tool. See and hear practical applications of MIDI gear: keyboards, sound modules, effect processors, recorders, mixers, triggers, and controllers.
©2002, softcover with CD, $14.95
ISBN #1-931140-28-6

---

www.artistpro.com—toll free 866 649-2665—or visit your favorite retailer.

artistpro.com, LLC
236 Georgia St., Suite 100
Vallejo, CA 94590
707 554-1935

ProAudio Press is an imprint of artistpro.com, LLC

DISTRIBUTED BY
HAL•LEONARD CORPORATION
7777 W. BLUEMOUND RD. P.O. BOX 13819 MILWAUKEE, WI 53213